Hungry Hedgehog

Hungry Hedgehog is looking for food.

3

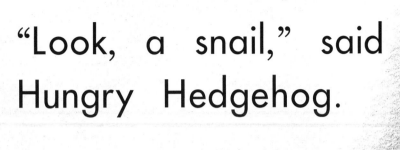

"Look, a snail," said
Hungry Hedgehog.

Hungry Hedgehog
likes snails.

4

"Look, a worm," said Hungry Hedgehog.

Hungry Hedgehog likes worms.

"Look, a beetle," said
Hungry Hedgehog.

Hungry Hedgehog
likes beetles.

9

"Look, an egg," said Hungry Hedgehog.

Hungry Hedgehog likes eggs.

"Look, cat food," said Hungry Hedgehog.

Hungry Hedgehog likes cat food.

13

"Go away,
Hungry Hedgehog!"
said the cat.

15

"This is my food!"

16